Praying the Scriptures

For Help, Hope & Healing

VELMA LYONS BARR

ENTEGRITY
CHOICE PUBLISHING

Entegrity Choice Publishing
PO Box 453 Powder Springs, GA 30127
info@entegritypublishing.com
www.entegritypublishing.com
404.472.9190

Printed in the United States of America

ISBN: 979-8-9850792-6-5

Library of Congress Control Number: 2024903938

Acknowledgments

First, I thank my Lord and Savior, Jesus Christ, for the publishing of this book. To God be all the glory!

To my loving husband, I love you more than words can say. Thank you so much for your support and love.

To my children, Ebony, Natadra, and Kendrick, I love you all so much, and I am so blessed to have such loving, amazing, respectful children. God gave you all to me, and I'm so glad He did.

To my grandchildren, Janiya, Jovan Jr., Zariya, Lennox, Chase, and Jace, you bring me so much love, laughter, and joy. I love you so much. Thank God for you all.

To my daughter-in-law, Briana, I love you very much. Thank God for you. My son is truly blessed.

To my sons-in-law, whom I love so much, thank God for both of you. Jovan Jones and Courtland Harden are gifts from God. My daughters are truly blessed.

I thank God for my family, whom I love so much. You are in my prayers. I will continue to cover you all because I know prayer changes things, and prayer is the answer. #BLESS FAMILY!

I am thankful for the missionaries of Fort Lauderdale,

Florida, who poured into my life concerning prayer and living holy. Missionary Evangelist Spence, Missionary Jackson, Missionary Wright, Missionary Corker, Missionary Tanniehill, Missionary Jan, Missionary Rhodes, Missionary Lawton, and Missionary Brown (RIP), I love you all. I'm forever grateful to you.

Dedication

To My Parents
Willie Lyons & Rose J. Wilson

Dad, you had a big heart. You would cook and feed not just your children but anyone who asked, "Willie, what do you have to eat?" Some people couldn't even walk straight, and it didn't matter to you. You made sure they got something to eat.

I miss you, but I know you're in a better place with no more pain. The day you prayed with me and said yes to God was definitely a day of rejoicing. 1 Samuel 16: 7b says, "For the Lord sees not as man sees; for man looks on the outward appearance, but the Lord looks on the heart."

I will love you forever, Dad. I know heaven is phenomenal.

Mom, you had great faith. You were a praying woman. Ann, Debra, Sally, and I heard you praying every morning. Sometimes you cried out to God. We didn't understand what you were doing at the time, but as we got older, we knew we had a praying mom. You prayed in the morning and at night, and you passed the mantle down to each of us.

I will never forget the time I said to you, "Mom, you

have a scripture pinned to your bra," and you replied, "I'm sleeping on the Word." You also put scriptures in your shoes and told us that you were walking on the Word of God. The awakening you had before you left this earth was amazing to witness.

Mom, your presence is missed, but I know you're in a better place. Until we meet in that heavenly place with the streets paved with gold, remember that I love you!

Contents

Introduction

PRAYING GOD'S WORD will bring comfort, help, hope and healing in every area of your life.

> *"And Jesus answering said unto them, Have faith in God. For*
> *verily I say unto you, that whosoever shall say unto this mountain,*
> *Be thou removed, and be thou cast into the sea; and shall not*
> *doubt in his heart, but shall believe that those things which*
> *he saith shall come to pass; he shall have whatsoever he saith.*
> *Therefore I say unto you, What things soever you desire, when*
> *you pray, believe that you receive them, and ye shall have them."*
> —MARK 11:22–24 KJV

> *"And this is the confidence that we have in him that, if*
> *we ask any thing according to his will, he hears us: And*
> *if we know that he hear us, whatsoever we ask, we know*
> *that we have the petitions that we desired of him."*
> —1 JOHN 5:14–15 KJV

It is my prayer that you will be encouraged and inspired to stand on the promises of God's Word. Pray these scriptures by faith according to Isaiah 55:11 which says, "So shall my word be that goes forth out of My mouth; it shall not return unto me void, but it shall accomplish that which I please, and it shall prosper in the thing whereto I sent it."

Praying scriptures mixed with faith—
changes everything!

1

God Cares

HAVE YOU EVER FELT that no one really understood you, or really cared? Have you ever felt all alone in your sorrow? It is interesting how satan play his games in our minds. He seeks to make us feel that God does not care.

God continually calls us to come to him with our burdens and find rest for our souls. He invites us to cast our worries on him because he cares. He invites us to come to his throne and ask for mercy and grace to help us in our time of need. He will be our Comforter in sorrow when our heart is faint. He offers strength when we are weak. He heals the broken hearted and binds up their wounds.

> *"Casting the whole of your care, all your anxieties, all your worries, all your concerns, once and for all on Him, for He cares for you affectionately and cares about you watchfully."*
> —I PETER 5:7 AMPC

*"Cast your burden on the Lord [release it] and He will sustain you:
He will never allow the righteous to be shaken (slip, fall, fail)."*
—PSALM 55:22 AMP

"Depend on the LORD; trust him, and he will take care of you."
—PSALM 37:5 NCV

*"Keep your lives free from the love of money, and be
satisfied with what you have. For God has said, "I
will never leave you; I will never abandon you."*
—HEBREWS 13:5 GNT

"Surely God is my help; the Lord is the one who sustains me."
—PSALM 54:4 NIV

*"After these things the word of the LORD came to
Abram in a vision: Fear not, Abram, I am your
shield; your reward shall be very great."*
—GENESIS 15:1 ESV

*"I am the good shepherd. The good shepherd
lays down his life for the sheep."*
—JOHN 10:11 NIV

*"He who did not spare his own Son, but delivered him up for us
all, how shall he not with him also freely give us all things?"*
—ROMANS 8:32 KJV

2

You Are Never Alone

THERE IS NO REASON TO FEAR; you are not alone. God admonishes us not to be discouraged because he goes before us and will be with us. God has the power to do jaw-dropping amazing things in our lives! He wants us to fulfill the purpose and plan He has for us, and we have the help of the Holy Spirit to do it. We need to keep moving forward, trusting God to help us.

"Have I not commanded you? Be strong and courageous!
Do not be terrified or dismayed (intimidated), for the
LORD your God is with you wherever you go."
—JOSHUA 1:9 AMP

"I repeat, be strong and brave! Don't be afraid and don't panic,
for I, the LORD your God, am with you in all you do."
—JOSHUA 1:9 NET

"Have I not given you your orders? Take heart and
be strong; have no fear and do not be troubled; for
the Lord your God is with you wherever you go."
—JOSHUA 1:9 BBE

"This is my command, be strong and courageous!
Do not be afraid or discouraged. For the LORD
your God is with you wherever you go."
—JOSHUA 1:9 NLT

"Remember that I commanded you to be strong and
brave. Don't be afraid, because the LORD your
God will be with you everywhere you go."
—JOSHUA 1:9 NCV

"Above all, be strong and very courageous to observe
carefully the whole instruction my servant Moses
commanded you. Do not turn from it to the right or the
left, so that you will have success wherever you go."
—JOSHUA 1:7 CSB

"The LORD is my light and my salvation; whom shall I fear? the
LORD is the strength of my life; of whom shall I be afraid?"
—PSALM 27:1 KJV

"Just as I was with Moses, I will be with you. No
one will be able to stop you all your life. I will
not abandon you. I will never leave you."
—JOSHUA 1:5 ERV

3

God Is Good

GOD IS GOOD in so many ways—the way he provides for us, guides us, and watches over us—but it goes even deeper than that. God's goodness is who he is, and we are created in his image, so, therefore, we share his goodness.

God's goodness is demonstrated in our lives every single day. Although we often think of his goodness when something big happens, his goodness abounds all the time—in every second, minute and hour of the day, in the smallest of things around us.

"O taste and see that the Lord [our God] is good;
How blessed [fortunate, prosperous, and favored by
God] is the man who takes refuge in Him."
—PSALM 34:8 AMP

"How sweet are thy words unto my taste! yea,
sweeter than honey to my mouth!"
—PSALM 119:103 KJV

"How priceless is your unfailing love, O God! People take refuge in the shadow of your wings."
—PSALM 36:7 NIV

"Pour out your unfailing love on those who love you; give justice to those with honest hearts."
—PSALM 36:10 NLT

"O give thanks to the LORD, for He is good; For His compassion and lovingkindness endure forever!"
—PSALM 107:1 AMP

4

Fear Not

THE LORD IS BIGGER than any problem or situation we can ever face. He reminds us through his word that he will strengthen, help, and hold us up with his victorious right hand.

The next time fear rises, turn your attention to God's promises. Turn your spirit to His. Ignite your faith by prayer and reading His Word. Replace every fearful thought with Scripture because God is bigger than our fears. Do not panic...there is no need to fear.

> *"Be strong. Take courage. Don't be intimidated. Don't*
> *give them a second thought because GOD, your God,*
> *is striding ahead of you. He's right there with you.*
> *He won't let you down; he won't leave you."*
> —DEUTERONOMY 31:6 MSG

"God is our refuge and strength, an ever—present help in trouble. Therefore we will not fear, though the earth give way and the mountains falls into the heart of the sea, though its waters roar and foam and mountains quake with their surging."

—PSALM 46:1–3 ICB

"Surely God is my salvation; I will trust and not be afraid. The LORD, the LORD himself, is my strength and my defense; he has become my salvation."

—ISAIAH 12:2 NIV

"For I am the LORD your God who takes hold of your right hand and says to you, Do not fear; I will help you."

—ISAIAH 41:13

"When thou passeth through the waters, I will be with thee; and through the rivers, they shall not overflow thee: when thou walkest through the fire, thou shalt not be burned; neither shall the flame kindle upon thee."

—ISAIAH 43:2 KJV

"I, I am he that comforts you; who are you that you are afraid of man who dies, of the son of man who is made like grass."

—ISAIAH 51:12 RSV

"For God hath not given us the spirit of fear; but of power, love and of a sound mind."

—2 TIMOTHY 1:7 KJV

"There is no fear in love; but perfect love casteth out fear: because fear hath torment. He that feareth is not made perfect in love."
—I JOHN 4:18 KJV

"Then David said to Solomon his son, "Be strong and courageous and do it. Do not be afraid and do not be dismayed, for the LORD God, even my God, is with you. He will not leave you or forsake you, until all the work for the service of the house of the LORD is finished."
—I CHRONICLES 28:20 ESV

5

When You Are Distressed

THE DEMANDS AND PRESSURES we face can often leave us feeling overwhelmed and anxious. In such times, finding solace in the Scriptures of the Bible can bring comfort and guidance.

The Scriptures offer wisdom, encouragement, and assurance, reminding us of God's love and the peace He offers amidst the storms of life.

God understands our struggles and offers His help and guidance. *"For my yoke is easy and my burden is light."* These comforting words from Jesus remind us to seek His presence when we are feeling overwhelmed, for He offers rest and relief from our burdens.

> *"Then Jesus said, "Come to me, all of you who are weary and carry heavy burdens, and I will give you rest. Take my yoke upon you. Let me teach you, because I am humble and gentle at heart, and you will find rest for your souls. For my yoke is easy to bear, and the burden I give you is light."*
> —MATTHEW 11:28–30 NLT

*"I have set the LORD always before me: because he
is at my right hand, I shall not be moved."*
—PSALM 16:8 KJV

*"In my distress I called upon the LORD and cried
to my God: and he did hear my voice out of his
temple, and my cry did enter into his ear."*
—2 SAMUEL 22:7 KJV

*"Why am I discouraged? Why is my heart so sad? I
will put my hope in God! I will praise him again."*
—PSALM 42:5 NLT

*"For I know the plans I have for you, declares the LORD,
plans to prosper you and not to harm you, plans to give
you hope and a future. Then you will call upon me and
come and pray to me, and I will listen to you."*
—JEREMIAH 29:11–12 NIV

*"I pray that God, the source of hope, will fill you completely with
joy and peace because you trust in him. Then you will overflow
with confident hope through the power of the Holy Spirit."*
—ROMANS 15:13 NLT

*"Incline your ear and come unto me: hear, and your
soul shall live; and I will make an everlasting covenant
with you, even the sure mercies of David."*
—ISAIAH 55:3 KJV

6

When You Need Strength

IN EVERY SEASON OF LIFE, we can find answers and direction in the Bible. When hard times make us feel weak or depleted, Bible verses about strength can heal and fortify our souls. Strength comes from God and our faith in him.

Psalm 46:1-3 (NIV) reminds us that "God is our refuge and strength, an ever-present help in trouble. Therefore, we will not fear, though the earth give way and the mountains fall into the heart of the sea, though its waters roar and foam and the mountains quake with their surging."

> "He gives strength to the weary, And to him who has no might
> He increases power. Even youths grow weary and tired, And
> vigorous young men stumble badly, But those who wait for the
> LORD [who expect, look for, and hope in Him] Will gain new
> strength and renew their power; They will lift up their wings [and
> rise up close to God] like eagles [rising toward the sun]; They will
> run and not become weary, They will walk and not grow tired."
>
> —ISAIAH 40:29-31 AMP

"Look to the LORD and His strength; seek his face always."
—I CHRONICLES 16:11 NIV

"The LORD is my strength and my shield; my heart trusted in him, and I am helped: therefore my heart greatly rejoiceth; and with my song will praise him."
—PSALM 28:7 KJV

"The LORD delivers and vindicates me! I fear no one! The LORD protects my life! I am afraid of no one!"
—PSALM 27:1 NET

"God is our refuge and strength, a very present help in trouble."
—PSALM 46:1 KJV

"I can do all things through Christ which strengtheneth me."
—PHILIPPIANS 4:13 KJV

"The LORD is my strength and my song; he has given me victory. This is my God, and I will praise him—my father's God, and I will exalt him!"
—EXODUS 15:2 NLT

"Have no fear, for I am with you; do not be looking about in trouble, for I am your God; I will give you strength, yes, I will be your helper, yes, my true right hand will be your support."
—ISAIAH 41:10 BBE

"He gives power to the faint, and to him who has no might he increases strength. Even youths shall faint and be weary, and young men shall fall exhausted; but they who wait for the LORD shall renew their strength; they shall mount up with wings like eagles; they shall run and not be weary; they shall walk and not faint."

—ISAIAH 40:29–31 ESV

7

Trust God

TRUSTING GOD IS vital to our relationship with Him. We live in unprecedented times. We need to be reminded that God is in control and trustworthy, even if everything seems out of control. God knows what is going on—all the how's, when's and why's. When we do not know what to do or what will happen next, trust that He does.

God sees everything that is going on in our lives. We do not need to give in to fear. It is not easy, but we can remain confident in His word.

"Trust God from the bottom of your heart; don't try to figure out everything on your own. Listen for God's voice in everything you do, everywhere you go; he's the one who will keep you on track."
—PROVERBS 3:5–6 MSG

"Put all your hope in God, not looking to your reason for support. In all your ways give ear to him, and he will make straight your footsteps."
—PROVERBS 3:5–6 BBE

"It is better to trust in the LORD than to put confidence in man."
—PSALM 118:8 KJV

"Don't put your confidence in powerful people;
there is no help for you there."
—PSALM 146:3 NLT

"Thus saith the LORD; Cursed be the man that
trusteth in man, and maketh flesh his arm, and
whose heart departed from the LORD."
—JEREMIAH 17:5 KJV

"He that trusted in his riches shall fall: but the
righteous shall flourish as a branch."
—PROVERBS 11:28 KJV

"He that trusteth in his own heart is a fool: but
whoso walketh wisely, he shall be delivered."
—PROVERBS 28:26 KJV

"Trust in the LORD, and do good; so shalt thou dwell in the land,
and verily thou shalt be fed. Delight thyself also in the LORD;
and he shall give thee the desires of thine heart. Commit thy way
unto the LORD; trust also in him; and he shall bring it to pass."
—PSALM 37:3–5 KJV

"I will instruct thee and teach thee in the way which
thou shalt go I will guide thee with mine eye."
—PSALM 32:8 KJV

8

Blessing of The Lord

O NE OF THE GREATEST blessings we have received is the
Holy Spirit, in whom we were sealed on the day of
our salvation. It is through the Holy Spirit that we receive
blessings of His presence, His help, His provision, and His
comfort. Throughout the Bible we are reminded of God's
past, present, and future blessings. For those that are willing
and obedient, they shall eat the good of the land.

God can pour on the blessings in astonishing ways, so
that you are ready for anything and everything, more than
just ready to do what needs to be done.

*"And God is able to provide you with every blessing in
abundance, so that you may always have enough of everything
and may provide in abundance for every good work."*
—2 CORINTHIANS 9:8 RSV

*"Being enriched in every thing to all bountifulness,
which causeth through us thanksgiving to God."*
—2 CORINTHIANS 9:11 KJV

"The blessing of the LORD, it maketh rich,
and he addeth no sorrow with it."
—PROVERBS 10:22 KJV

"The silver is mine, and the gold is mine,
declares the Lord of hosts."
—HAGGAI 2:8 KJV

"The earth is the LORD'S and the fulness thereof;
the world, and they that dwell therein."
—PSALM 24:1 KJV

"Both riches and honour come of thee, and thou reignest
over all; and in thine hand is power and might; and in thine
hand it is to make great, and to give strength unto all."
—I CHRONICLES 29:12 KJV

"The LORD shall open unto thee his good treasure, the
heaven to give the rain unto thy land in his season, and
to bless all the work of thine hand: and thou shalt lend
unto many nations, and thou shalt not borrow."
—DEUTERONOMY 28:12 KJV

"Bring ye all the tithes into the storehouse, that there may be meat
in mine house, and prove me now herewith, saith the LORD of
hosts, if I will not open you the windows of heaven, and pour you
out a blessing, that there shall not be room enough to receive it."
—MALACHI I 3:10 KJV

"For the LORD God is a sun and shield: the LORD will give grace and glory: no good thing will he withhold from them that walk uprightly."

—PSALM 84:11 KJV

Don't Worry About Anything

GOD DOES NOT want us to focus on things that are outside of our control. God wants us to trust him instead of reflecting on worrisome things. We have victory through Jesus Christ in every situation.

In the end we know that all things work together for good to them that love God, to them who are called according to his purpose. Satan would love nothing more than to keep us in a state of anxiety, doubt, and fear. Think Jesus!

> *"And the peace of God, which passeth all understanding,*
> *shall keep your hearts and minds through Christ Jesus."*
> —PHILIPPIANS 4:7 KJV

> *"Give all your worries and cares to God, for he cares about you."*
> —I PETER 5:7 NLT

*"Don't worry about anything, but in everything, through prayer
and petition with thanksgiving, present your requests to God.
And the peace of God, which surpasses all understanding,
will guard your hearts and minds in Christ Jesus."*
—PHILIPPIANS 4:6–7 CSB

*"That is why I tell you not to worry about everyday life—whether
you have enough food and drink, or enough clothes to wear. Isn't
life more than clothing? Look at the birds. They don't plant or
harvest or store food in barns, for heavenly Father feeds them.
And aren't you far more valuable to him than they are? Can
all your worries add a single moment to your life? Look at the
lilies of the field and how they grow. They don't work or make
their clothing, yet Solomon in all his glory was not dressed
as beautifully as they are. And if God cares so wonderfully
for wildflowers that are here today and thrown into the fire
tomorrow, he will certainly care for you. Why do you have so
little faith? So don't worry about these things, saying, 'What will
we eat? What will we drink? What will we wear?' These things
dominate the thoughts of unbelievers, but your heavenly Father
already knows all your needs. Seek the kingdom of God above
all else, and live righteously, and he will give you everything
you need. So don't worry about tomorrow, for tomorrow will
bring its own worries. Today's trouble is enough for today."*
—MATTHEW 6:25–34 NLT

"Don't fret or worry. Instead of worrying, pray. Let petitions and praises shape your worries into prayers, letting God know your concerns. Before you know it, a sense of God's wholeness, everything coming together for good, will come and settle you down. It's wonderful what happens when Christ displaces worry at the center of your life."
—PHILIPPIANS 4:6–7 MSG

10

God's Protection

THE BIBLE IS FILLED with God's promises to protect us. These promises are powerful enough that they can be applied to a variety of life's struggles—and sometimes you may find a single promise that speaks so strongly to you, that it helps you shore up your spirit against more than one challenge in your life—making these words a powerful balm in times of crisis.

> *"God is a safe place to hide, ready to help when we need him. We stand fearless at the cliff edge of doom, courageous in seastorm and earthquake. Before the rush and roar of oceans, the tremors that shift mountains. Jacob—wrestling God fights for us, God-of-Angels-Armies protects us."*
> —PSALM 46:1–3 MSG

> *"But the Lord is faithful, and he will strengthen you and protect you from the evil one. We have confidence in the Lord that you are*

doing and will continue to do the things we command. May the Lord direct your hearts into God's love and Christ's perseverance."
—2 THESSALONIANS 3:3–5 NIV

"No weapon that is formed against thee shall prosper; and every tongue that shall rise against thee in judgement thou shalt condemn. This is the heritage of the servants of the LORD, and their righteousness is of me, saith the LORD."
—ISAIAH 54:17 KJV

"And the Lord shall deliver me from every evil work and will preserve me unto his heavenly kingdom: to whom be glory for ever and ever. Amen"
—2 TIMOTHY 4:18 KJV

"Though I walk in the mist of trouble, thou wilt revive me: Thou shalt stretch forth thine hand against the wrath of mine enemies, and thy right hand shall save me."
—PSALM 138:7 KJV

"God is our refuge and strength, always ready to help in times of trouble."
—PSALM 46:1 NLT

"So that we may boldly say, The Lord is my helper, and I will not fear what man shall do unto me."
—HEBREWS 13:6 KJV

"Take up God's instruments of war, so that you may be able to keep your position against all the deceit of the Evil One."

—EPHESIANS 6:11 BBE

11

The Good Shepherd

IN JESUS' DESCRIPTION of Himself in John 10 he adds to our understanding of what makes for a good shepherd. The good shepherd is sacrificial. He is willing to ignore his own needs in order to meet the needs of the sheep. Over and over in the passage he states the good shepherd gives his own life for his sheep.

To say, "The Lord is my shepherd," does not mean that I own Him but that He owns me. The shepherd owns the sheep; they are his property. They are not wild animals like wolves. He purchases them at a price and cares for them with love.

> "The LORD is my Shepherd [to feed, to guide and to
> shield me], I shall not want. He lets me lie down in green
> pastures; He leads me beside the still and quiet waters.
> He refreshes and restores my soul (life); He leads me
> in the paths of righteousness for His name's sake.

Even though I walk through the [sunless] valley of the shadow of death, I fear no evil, for You are with me; Your rod [to protect] and Your staff [to guide], they comfort and console me. You prepare a table before me in the presence of my enemies. You have anointed and refreshed my head with oil; My cup overflows.

Surely goodness and mercy and unfailing love shall follow me all the days of my life, And I shall dwell forever [throughout all my days] in the house and in the presence of the Lord."

—PSALM 23 AMP

12

Love

GOD SO LOVED THE WORLD that he gave his only begotten son. God's love for us moved Him to send his only son for the world's redemption. Jesus Christ's perfect, unconditional love was evident when he sacrificed himself on the cross for the sins of the world.

Faith involves trusting that at the center of the universe is a being overflowing with love for his world, which means that the purpose of human existence is to receive this love that has come to us in Jesus and then to give it back out to others.

"Love endures with patience and serenity, love is kind and thoughtful, and is not jealous or envious; love does not brag and is not proud or arrogant. It is not rude; it is not self-seeking, it is not provoked [nor overly sensitive and easily angered]; it does not take into account a wrong endured. It does not rejoice at injustice, but rejoices with the truth [when right and truth prevail]. Love bears all things [regardless of what comes], believes all things [looking for the best in each one], hopes all things

[remaining steadfast during difficult times], endures all things [without weakening]. Love never fails [it never fades nor ends]. But as for prophecies, they will pass away; as for tongues, they will cease; as for the gift of special knowledge, it will pass away."
—I CORINTHIANS 13:4–8 AMP

13

The Grace of God

GRACE IS THE MOST IMPORTANT concept taught in the Bible. The bible is filled with scriptures about God's grace, and even though it is not something we deserve, God is kind to us and wants the best for our lives. Simply put—grace is the unmerited, unearned love and favor of God.

"But by the grace of God, I am what I am, and His grace toward me was not in vain. On the contrary, I worked harder than any of them, though it was not I but the grace of God that is with me."
—I CORINTHIANS 15:10 ICB

"Let us, then, feel free to come before God's throne. Here there is grace. And we can receive mercy and grace to help us when we need it."
—HEBREWS 4:16 ICB

"God saved you by his grace when you believed. And you can't take credit for this; it is a gift from God."
—EPHESIANS 2:8 NLT

"And He said to me, "My grace is sufficient for you,
for My strength is made perfect in weakness."
—2 CORINTHIANS 12:9A NKJV

"Sin is no longer your master, for you no longer
live under the requirements of the law. Instead,
you live under the freedom of God's grace."
—ROMANS 6:14 NLT

"Let us therefore come boldly unto the throne of grace, that we
may obtain mercy, and find grace to help in time of need."
—HEBREWS 4:16 KJV

"For from his fulness we have all received, grace upon grace."
—JOHN 1:16 ESV

"Out of the fullness of his grace he has blessed us
all, giving us one blessing after another."
—JOHN 1:16 GLT W/APOCRYPHA

14

When You Feel Like Giving Up

THE LORD LISTENS to his people when they call to him for help. He rescues them from all their troubles. The Lord is close to the brokenhearted; he rescues those whose spirits are crushed.

We must trust in God's Word. The Bible says that God cannot lie. He always keeps His promises. Having faith in God during difficult times can allow you to find peace.

"And let us not be weary in well doing for in due
season we shall reap, if we faint not."
—GALATIANS 6:9 KJV

"God is our refuge and strength, a very present help in trouble."
—PSALM 46:1 KJV

"Think of all the hostility he endured from sinful people;
then you won't become weary and give up."
—HEBREWS 12:3 NLT

"The LORD is my strength and my shield; my heart trusted in him, and I am helped: therefore my heart greatly rejoiceth; and with my song will I praise him."
—PSALM 28:7 KJV

"All that the Father giveth me shall come to me; and him that cometh to me I will in no wise cast out."
—JOHN 6:37 KJV

"Being confident of this very thing, that he which hath begun a good work in you will perform it until the day of Jesus Christ."
—PHILIPPIANS 1:6 KJV

"Let your conversation be without covetousness; and be content with such things as ye have: for he hath said, I will never leave thee, nor forsake thee."
—HEBREWS 13:5 KJV

"Dear brothers and sisters, when troubles come your way, consider it an opportunity for great joy. For you know that when your faith is tested, your endurance has a chance to grow. So let it grow, for when your endurance is fully developed, you will be perfect and complete, needing nothing. If you need wisdom, ask our generous God, and he will give it to you. He will not rebuke you for asking."
—JAMES 1:2–5 NLT

"Because of our faith, Christ has brought us into this place of undeserved privilege where we now stand, and we confidently and joyfully look forward to sharing God's glory. We can rejoice, too, when we run into problems and trials, for we know that they help us develop endurance. And endurance develops strength of character, and character strengthens our confident hope of salvation."

—ROMANS 5:2–4 NLT

15

Hope

HOPE CARRIES NO DOUBT. Hope is a sure foundation upon which we base our lives, believing that God always keeps His promises. Hope can be ours when we trust the words, "He who believes on Me has everlasting life."

Accepting Jesus Christ means our hope is no longer filled with doubt but, rather, has at its sure foundation the whole of God's Word, the entirety of God's character, and the finished work of our Lord and Savior Jesus Christ.

When you need encouragement and refreshment for your soul, turn to the scriptures from the Old and New Testaments that offer hope and encouragement. Everyone needs to be reminded from time to time of the hope that God offers to us.

> *"Because of the Lord's great love we are not*
> *consumed, for his compassions never fail. They are*
> *new every morning; great is your faithfulness."*
> —LAMENTATIONS 3:21–23 NIV

"Now the God of hope fill you with all joy and peace in believing, that ye may abound in hope, through the power of the Holy Ghost."
—ROMANS 15:13 KJV

"The LORD values those who fear him, those who put their hope in his faithful love."
—PSALM 147:11 CSB

"Behold, the eye of the LORD is upon them that fear him; upon them that hope in his mercy;"
—PSALM 33:18 KJV

"Let thy mercy, O LORD, be upon us, according as we hope in thee."
—PSALM 33:22 KJV

"You keep track of all my sorrows. You have collected all my tears in your bottle. You have recorded each one in your book."
—PSALM 56:8 NLT

"The name of the LORD is a strong tower; a righteous person rushes to it and is lifted up above the danger."
—PROVERBS 18:10 ISV

"May the God of hope fill you with all joy and peace as you trust in him, so that you may overflow with hope by the power of the Holy Spirit."
—ROMANS 15:13 NIV

"For I know the thoughts that I think toward you, saith the LORD, thoughts of peace, and not of evil, to give you an expected end."
—JEREMIAH 29:11 KJV

16

Confidence

T HE BIBLE IS FILLED WITH SCRIPTURES to bolster your confidence and self-esteem. God loves us, and He wants us to love ourselves. He wants us to see ourselves the way He sees us. The Bible teaches us to put our identity in the Lord alone. When He is the source of our worth, we can stand tall in our true identities. Let these Bible verses on confidence inspire you and give you life.

"I can do all things through Christ which strengthen me."
—PHILIPPIANS 4:13 KJV

*"Cast not away therefore your confidence, which
hath great recompence of reward."*
—HEBREWS 10:35 KJV

*"And this is the confidence that we have in him, that if
we ask anything according to his will, he heareth us:"*
—I JOHN 5:14 KJV

*"For God hath not given us the spirit of fear; but
of power, and of love, and of a sound mind."*
—2 TIMOTHY 1:7 KJV

*"Though a host should encamp against me, my heart shall not
fear: though war should rise against me, in this will I be confident."*
—PSALM 27:3 KJV

*"And whatsoever we ask, we receive of him, because we keep his
commandments, and those things that are pleasing in his sight."*
—1 JOHN 3:22 KJV

*"I praise you because I am fearfully and wonderfully made;
your works are wonderful, I know that full well."*
—PSALM 139:14 NIV

*"But he said to me, "My grace is sufficient for you,
for my power is made perfect in weakness." Therefore
I will boast all the more gladly about my weaknesses,
so that Christ's power may rest on me."*
—2 CORINTHIANS 12:9 NIV

*"In him and through faith in him we may approach
God with freedom and confidence."*
—EPHESIANS 3:12 NIV

17

Peace

WHEN TIMES GET TOUGH, it can be difficult to find
peace. You may be going through some challenges and
hard times right now, whether you are experiencing financial
struggles, personal difficulties, health problems, or a sense of
anxiety at the state of the world. When you are struggling to
find peace, the words of the Bible can help you find comfort
and healing.

> *"Thou wilt keep him in perfect peace, whose mind*
> *is stayed on thee: because he trusteth in thee."*
> —ISAIAH 26:3 KJV

> *"And the peace of God, which passeth all understanding,*
> *shall keep your hearts and minds through Christ Jesus."*
> —PHILIPPIANS 4:7 KJV

> *"And let the peace of God rule in your hearts, to the which*
> *also ye are called in one body; and be ye thankful."*
> —COLOSSIANS 3:15 KJV

*"You keep completely safe the people who
maintain their faith, for they trust in you."*
—ISAIAH 26:3 NET

*"I create the fruit of the lips: Peace, peace to him that is far off
and to him who is near," Says the LORD, "And I will heal him."*
—ISAIAH 57:19 NKJV

*"I have told you all this so that you may have peace in
me, Here on earth you will have many trails and sorrows.
But take heart, because I have overcome the world."*
—JOHN 16:33 NLT

*"Peace I leave with you; my peace I give to you; not
as the world gives do I give to you. Let not your
hearts be troubled, neither let them be afraid."*
—JOHN 14:27 RSV

18

How to Handle Relationships

HEALTHY RELATIONSHIPS are so important that God didn't just suggest we treat others well; He commanded it. Colossians 3:13 says, "Bear with each other and forgive whatever grievances you may have against one another. Forgive as the Lord forgave you."

To "bear with" means to give lots of grace and not to be easily offended. And forgive whatever grievances you have, regardless of how offended you are or how right you are. The most important commandment Jesus gave us is to love God and love others.

> *"Love from the center of who you are; don't fake it. Run for*
> *dear life from evil; hold on for dear life to good. Be good*
> *friends who love deeply; practice playing second fiddle."*
> —ROMANS 12:9–10 MSG

"Above all, have fervent and unfailing love for one another,
because love covers a multitude of sins [it overlooks
unkindness and unselfishly seeks the best for others]."

—1 PETER 4:8 AMP

"When you talk, do not say harmful things. But say what
people need—words that will help others become stronger.
Then what you say will help those who listen to you."

—EPHESIANS 4:29 ICB

"Don't just pretend to love others. Really love them. Hate what
is wrong. Hold tightly to what is good. Love each other with
genuine affection, and take delight in honoring each other."

—ROMANS 12:9–10 NLT

"Dear children, let's not merely say that we love each
other; let us show the truth by our actions. Our actions will
show that we belong to the truth, so we will be confident
when we stand before God. Even if we feel guilty, God is
greater than our feelings, and he knows everything."

—1 JOHN 3:18–20 NLT

"Now about your love for one another we do
not need to write to you, for you yourselves have
been taught by God to love each other."

—1 THESSALONIANS 4:9 NIV

"Do not seek revenge or bear a grudge against anyone among
your people, but love your neighbor as yourself. I am the Lord."

—LEVITICUS 19:18 NIV

19

What to Do When You Are Discouraged

JESUS DOES NOT WANT US TO BE DISCOURAGED. In fact, he commands us not to be. Listen to what Jesus says to his disciples just before what probably was the most discouraging experience of their lives—his brutal death: "Let not your hearts be troubled."

No matter how many times we are beaten down, no matter what discriminations and hardships we face, we will always stand up and rise to meet another day because he gives us the strength to do so. Do not be discouraged.

> *"Why are you down in the dumps, dear soul? Why are you crying the blues? Fix my eyes on God—soon I'll be praising again. He put a smile on my face. He's my God."*
> —PSALM 42:11 MSG

> *"Is anyone crying for help? GOD is listening, ready to rescue you. If your heart is broken, you'll find GOD right there; if you're kicked in the gut, he'll help you catch your breath."*
> —PSALM 34:17–18 MSG

"Has anyone by fussing before the mirror ever gotten taller by so much as an inch? If fussing can't even do that, why fuss at all?"
—LUKE 12:25–26 MSG

"Always be humble and gentle. Be patient with each other, making allowance for each other's faults because of your love."
—EPHESIANS 4:2 NLT

"I waited and waited and waited for GOD. At last he looked; finally he listened. He lifted me out of the ditch, pulled me from deep mud. He stood me up on a solid rock to make sure I wouldn't slip."
—PSALMS 40:1–2 MSG

20

Healing Belongs to You

READING THE BIBLE HEALS YOU because it reminds you of God's love and His power to heal the sick. Whether physical, mental, or emotional, God can heal your illnesses.

In life, we encounter many kinds of illnesses and problems. Sometimes, we cannot get through it by ourselves, whether it's sickness, grief, or sadness. It is easy to get stuck and feel like there's no way out. Happily, you are never alone through these tough times—God is always with you.

When you feel weak, these Bible verses may help you find the comfort and strength you need.

> *"But he was wounded for our transgressions, he was bruised for our iniquities: the chastisement of our peace was upon him; and with his stripes we are healed."*
> —ISAIAH 53:5 KJV

> *"O Lord my God, I pleaded with you, and you gave me my health again."*
> —PSALM 30:2 TLB

"He himself bore our sins" in his body on the cross, so that we might die to sins and live for righteousness; "by his wounds you have been healed." For "you were like sheep going astray," but now you have returned to the Shepherd and Overseer of your souls."
—I PETER 2:24–25 NIV

"For I will restore health to you, and your wounds I will heal, declares the Lord, because they have called you an outcast: 'It is Zion, for whom no one cares!' "
—JEREMIAH 30:17 ESV

"I have seen what they do, but I will heal them anyway! I will lead them. I will comfort those who mourn, bringing words of praise to their lips."
—ISAIAH 57:18 NLT

"Let all that I am praise the LORD; may I never forget the good things he does for me. He forgives all my sins and heals all my diseases. He redeems me from death and crowns me with love and tender mercies. He fills my life with good things. My youth is renewed like the eagle's!"
—PSALM 103:2–5 NLT

"But I will restore you to health and heal your wounds, declares the Lord, because you are called an outcast, Zion for whom no one cares."
—JEREMIAH 30:17 NIV

"Confess your faults one to another, and pray one for another, that ye may be healed. The effectual fervent prayer of a righteous man availeth much."
—JAMES 5:16 KJV

21

Give Thanks

THE HEBREW WORD thanksgiving is tôwdâh (to-daw') and it means confession, praise, and offering. When we give thanks in the truest sense of the biblical word, we offer God our praises and acknowledge to Him that He is the Giver of all good gifts. Our gratitude glorifies God as we exalt not the gifts, but the Giver. Gratitude helps us realize all we have comes not because of us, but from God.

> *"O give thanks to the Lord; call upon his name:*
> *make known his deeds among the people."*
> —PSALM 105:1 KJV

> *"Give thanks to the Lord because he is good. His love*
> *continues forever. Give thanks to the God over all*
> *gods. His love continues forever. Give thanks to the*
> *Lord of all lords. His love continues forever."*
> —PSALM 136:1-3 ICB

"In that wonderful day you will sing: Thank the Lord! Praise his name! Tell the nations what he has done. Let them know how mighty he is! Sing to the Lord, for he has done wonderful things. Make known his praise around the world."
—ISAIAH 12:4–5 NLT

"Give thanks to the Lord, for he is good! His faithful love endures forever."
—1 CHRONICLES 16:34 NLT

"And let the peace that comes from Christ rule in your hearts. For as members of one body you are called to live in peace. And always be thankful. Let the message about Christ, in all its richness, fill your lives. Teach and counsel each other with all the wisdom he gives. Sing psalms and hymns and spiritual songs to God with thankful hearts. And whatever you do or say, do it as a representative of the Lord Jesus, giving thanks through him to God the Father."
—COLOSSIANS 3:15–17 NLT

22

Love Your Enemies

Today's climate makes it easy to harbor feelings of resentment toward others or toward a specific group of people. This is especially true regarding social media and how we use it. We need to watch out for feelings of resentment because resentment can turn into hatred if we are not careful.

Since we are so divided, it can seem impossible to love your enemies. However, we need to stop hating one another because hating one another is the easy way out. To become more like Christ, we need to harness feelings of love and acceptance.

Many times, Jesus was betrayed and persecuted, and time and again, he chose forgiveness and understanding. Even when he was nailed to the cross, Jesus said, "Father, forgive them for they know not what they do."

"I say to you who are listening to me, love your enemies. Do good to those who hate you. Ask God to bless those who say bad things to you. Pray for those who are cruel to you."
—LUKE 6:27–28 ICB

"But you should do this: "If your enemy is hungry, feed him; if your enemy is thirsty, give him a drink. Doing this will be like pouring burning coals on his head. Do not let evil defeat you. Defeat evil by doing good."
—ROMANS 12:20–21 ICB

"You shall not take vengeance, nor bear any grudge against the children of your people, but you shall love your neighbor as yourself: I am the LORD."
—LEVITICUS 19:18 NKJV

"When a man's ways please the LORD, he maketh even his enemies to be at peace with him."
—PROVERBS 16:7 KJV

"Don't rejoice when your enemies fall; don't be happy when they stumble."
—PROVERBS 24:17 NLT

"If thine enemy be hungry, give him bread to eat; And if he be thirsty, give him water to drink: For thou wilt heap coals of fire upon his head, And Jehovah will reward thee."
—PROVERBS 25:21–22 ASV

"Love your enemies! Do good to them. Lend to them without expecting to be repaid. Then your reward from heaven will be very great, and you will truly be acting as children of the Most High, for he is kind to those who are unthankful and wicked."
—LUKE 6:35 NLT

"But I tell you, love your enemies and pray for those who persecuted you."
—MATTHEW 5:44 KJV

Don't say, "I will recompense evil;" Wait for the Lord, and He will save you.
—PROVERBS 20:22 NKJV

"Be kind to one another, tenderhearted, forgiving one another, as God in Christ forgave you."
—EPHESIANS 4:32 ESV

23

Encourage One Another

ENCOURAGEMENT IS SHARED with the hopes that it will lift someone's heart toward the Lord. *Pray for God to make you an encourager.* Ask him to give you a heart that loves others and creativity to know how to show it. Ask him to help you die to self-centeredness and grow in a desire to build others up. Because God delights in helping his people obey his commands, we can trust that his Spirit will teach us how to bless others for his glory and their spiritual good.

"When you talk, do not say harmful things. But say what
people need—words that will help others become stronger.
Then what you say will help those who listen to you."
—EPHESIANS 4:29 ICB

"Let the word of Christ dwell in you richly in all wisdom;
teaching and admonishing one another in psalms and hymns and
spiritual songs, singing with grace in your hearts to the Lord."
—COLOSSIANS 3:16 KJV

*"A wise person's heart makes his speech wise
and it adds persuasiveness to his words."*
—PROVERBS 16:23 NET

*"A man hath joy by the answer of his mouth: and a
word spoken in due season, how good is it."*
—PROVERBS 15:23 KJV

*"Everyone enjoys a fitting reply; it is wonderful
to say the right thing at the right time."*
—PROVERBS 15:23 NLT

24

Making Good Judgment

GOD WANTS US TO MAKE WISE DECISIONS, and he has given us an open invitation to ask for wisdom (James 1:5). We can be spared danger—entering unproductive relationships, pursuing unsuitable careers, sinking into debt, etc., by cherishing the sound judgment and spiritual discernment daily prayer brings to light.

We are to trust and seek God's leading as we wait for His direction. Psalm 143:8 tells us, "Let me hear your lovingkindness in the morning, for I trust in You. Teach me the way I should go for I lift up my soul to You."

"Get wisdom, get understanding; do not forget my words or turn away from them. Do not forsake wisdom, and she will protect you; love her, and she will watch over you. The beginning of wisdom is this: Get wisdom. Though it cost all you have, get understanding. Cherish her, and she will exalt you; embrace her, and she will honor you. She will give you a garland to grace your head and present you with a glorious crown." Listen, my

son, accept what I say, and the years of your life will be many.
I instruct you in the way of wisdom and lead you along straight
paths. When you walk, your steps will not be hampered; when
you run, you will not stumble. Hold on to instruction, do not
let it go; guard it well, for it is your life. Do not set foot on
the path of the wicked or walk in the way of evildoers. Avoid
it, do not travel on it; turn from it and go on your way."
—PROVERBS 4:5–15 KJV

"Trust in the Lord with all your heart, and do not lean on
your own understanding. In all your ways acknowledge
him, and he will make straight your paths."
—PROVERBS 3:5 ESV

"If you need wisdom, ask our generous God, and he will
give it to you. He will not rebuke you for asking."
—JAMES 1:5 NLT

25

Goodness of God

WHAT IS GOODNESS? Goodness is love in action and is perfected in God's giving and forgiving nature. Through His mercy, compassion and provision, God shows his goodness.

The goodness of the Lord is something that we can give thanks for daily! He shows loving-kindness, mercy, compassion, grace, and unfailing love to those who fear Him and who love His name. There are so many things to be grateful for as we think of God's goodness.

> *"Give thanks to the LORD, for he is good!*
> *His faithful love endures forever."*
> —PSALM 136:1 NLT

> *"I had fainted, unless I had believed to see the goodness*
> *of the LORD in the land of the living. Wait on the*
> *LORD: be of good courage, and he shall strengthen*
> *thine heart: wait, I say, on the LORD."*
> —PSALM 27:13-14 KJV

"If ye then, being evil, know how to give good gifts unto
your children, how much more shall your Father which
is in heaven give good things to them that ask him?"
—MATTHEW 7:11 KJV

"Oh how great is thy goodness, which thou hast laid up
for them that fear thee; which thou hast wrought for
them that trust in thee before the sons of men!"
—PSALM 31:19 KJV

"Let them give thanks to the Lord for his unfailing love
and his wonderful deeds for mankind, for he satisfies
the thirsty and fills the hungry with good things."
—PSALM 107:8–9 NIV

"Then Moses said, "Now show me your glory." And the Lord
said, "I will cause all my goodness to pass in front of you,
and I will proclaim my name, the Lord, in your presence.
I will have mercy on whom I will have mercy, and I will
have compassion on whom I will have compassion."
—EXODUS 33:18–19 NIV

26

Thanksgiving

THANKSGIVING MAGNIFIES GOD. It makes him great in the sense of declaring his greatness. Thanksgiving gives him the glory he deserves. It exalts him as the source of every good thing we enjoy.

The people of God are thankful people, for they realize how much they have been given. Thankfulness should be a way of life for us, naturally flowing from our hearts and mouths. We should be thankful because God is worthy of our thanksgiving.

> *"O give thanks unto the LORD; for he is good: For his mercy endureth for ever. O give thanks unto the God of gods: For his mercy endureth for ever. O give thanks to the Lord of lords: For his mercy endureth forever."*
> —PSALM 136:1–3 KJV

> *"Since everything God created is good, we should not reject any of it but receive it with thanks."*
> —1 TIMOTHY 4:4 NLT

"Delight thyself also in the Lord: and he shall give thee the desires of thine heart. Commit thy way unto the Lord; trust also in him; and he shall bring it to pass. And he shall bring forth thy righteousness as the light, and thy judgment as the noonday."
—PSALM 37:4–6 KJV

"Give thanks to the LORD, for he is good; his love endures forever."
—I CHRONICLES 16:34 NIV

"Rejoice always, pray continually, give thanks in all circumstances; for this is God's will for you in Christ Jesus."
—I THESSALONIANS 5:16–18 NIV

"Oh that men would praise the Lord for his goodness, and for his wonderful works to the children of men! For he satisfieth the longing soul, and filleth the hungry soul with goodness."
—PSALM 107:8–9 KJV

27

Patience

THE FRUIT OF PATIENCE is Inner Strength and Self-Control. Patience, as a fruit of the Holy Spirit, represents inner strength and self-control in the face of adversity, trials, and challenges. It enables believers to endure difficulties with grace and resilience, relying on the Holy Spirit's guidance and empowerment.

The fruit of the Spirit is love, joy, peace, patience, kindness, generosity, faithfulness, gentleness, self-control. Those who are in Christ are distinguished from unbelievers in that they have been gifted with the Holy Spirit, enabling them to bear fruit.

"Be joyful in hope, patient in affliction, faithful in prayer."
—ROMANS 12:12 NIV

"Be ye also patient; stablish your hearts: for
the coming of the Lord draweth nigh."
—JAMES 5:8 KJV

*"Whoever is patient has great understanding, but
one who is quick-tempered displays folly."*
—PROVERBS 14:29 NIV

*"Be completely humble and gentle; be patient,
bearing with one another in love."*
—EPHESIANS 4:2 NIV

*"Therefore, as God's chosen people, holy and
dearly loved, clothe yourselves with compassion,
kindness, humility, gentleness, and patience."*
—COLOSSIANS 3:12 NIV

*"The end of a matter is better than its beginning, and
patience is better than pride. Do not be quickly provoked
in your spirit, for anger resides in the lap of fools."*
—ECCLESIASTES 7:8–9 NIV

*"Be still before the LORD and wait patiently for
him; do not fret when people succeed in their ways,
when they carry out their wicked scheme."*
—PSALM 37:7 NIV

28

Choose Life

CHOOSING LIFE indicates that people have a choice, a decision to make. We choose life by choosing God. When we respond to the Lord in faith, love, and obedience, we receive life eternal. Jesus said, "I am the resurrection and the life. The one who believes in me will live."

We choose life when we accept Jesus Christ as our Lord and Savior and dedicate ourselves to following Him. He becomes our life. Our obedience to God brings life now in all its fullness, as well as life eternal.

> *"I call Heaven and Earth to witness against you today: I place*
> *before you Life and Death, Blessing and Curse. Choose life*
> *so that you and your children will live. And love God, your*
> *God, listening obediently to him, firmly embracing him."*
> —DEUTERONOMY 30:19–20 MSG

*"The Lord does not delay [as though He were unable to act]
and is not slow about His promise, as some count slowness,
but is [extraordinarily] patient toward you, not wishing
for any to perish but for all to come to repentance."*
—2 PETER 3:9 AMP

*"For God so loved the world, that he gave his only
begotten Son, that whosoever believeth in him
should not perish, but have everlasting life."*
—JOHN 3:16 KJV

*"Jesus said to him, "I am the [only] Way [to God]
and the [real] Truth and the [real] Life; no one
comes to the Father but through Me."*
—JOHN 14:6 AMP

29

Favor of God

FAVOR IS THE GRACE OF GOD IN OUR LIVES. In fact, the Old Testament often uses favor and grace interchangeably. The definition of grace is the unmerited favor of God, and favor means acceptance, goodwill, and preferential treatment. So, we can't earn favor and are never entitled to it.

God saved us because of His favor toward us. Ephesians 2:8 tells us, "For by grace you have been saved through faith, and that not of yourselves; it is the gift of God." Simply put, grace is favor. God's favor is the power that changes things for us.

> "For You, O LORD, bless the righteous man
> [the one who is in right standing with You]; You
> surround him with favor as with a shield."
> —PSALMS 5:12 AMP

"For the Lord God is a sun and shield; the Lord
bestows favor and honor; no good thing does he
withhold from those whose walk is blameless."
—PSALM 84:11 NIV

"For His anger endureth but a moment, and in his favor is life:
weeping may endure for a night, but joy cometh in the morning."
—PSALM 30:5 KJV

"For the Lord God is a sun and shield: the Lord
will give grace and glory: no good thing will he
withhold from them that walk uprightly."
—PSALM 84:11 KJV

"Remember me, O Lord, with the favour that thou bearest
unto thy people: O visit me with thy salvation;
—PSALM 106:4 KJV

"For by grace are ye saved through faith; and
that not of yourselves: it is the gift of God: Not
of works, lest any man should boast."
—EPHESIANS 2:8–9 KJV

30

Wisdom

"HOW MUCH BETTER to get wisdom than gold, to get insight rather than silver!" Wisdom in the Bible is worth a great deal, as scripture proclaims. This Bible verse about wisdom tells us that truth and insight are better than precious metals.

Wisdom is a God-given and God-centered discernment regarding the practical issues in life. Wisdom comes from prayer for God's help. God gives generously (with "single-minded" liberality) and without reproach (he does not want anyone to hesitate to come to him).

"If any of you lack wisdom, let him ask of God, that giveth to all men liberally, and upbraideth not; and it shall be given him."
—JAMES 1:5–7

"Trust in the Lord with all thine heart; and lean not unto thine own understanding. In all thy ways acknowledge him, and he shall direct thy paths."
—PROVERBS 3:5–6 KJV

"For the Lord giveth wisdom: out of his mouth cometh knowledge and understanding. He layeth up sound wisdom for the righteous: he is a buckler to them that walk uprightly. He keepeth the paths of judgment, and preserveth the way of his saints."
—PROVERBS 3:6–8 KJV

"Who is a wise man and endued with knowledge among you? let him shew out of a good conversation his works with meekness of wisdom. But if ye have bitter envying and strife in your hearts, glory not, and lie not against the truth. This wisdom descendeth not from above, but is earthly, sensual, devilish."
—JAMES 3:13–15 KJV

"Therefore whosoever heareth these sayings of mine, and doeth them, I will liken him unto a wise man, which built his house upon a rock:"
—MATTHEW 7:24 KJV

31

Insecurity

To be insecure is to lack confidence or trust, whether in ourselves or someone else. There are many causes of insecurity, but chief among them is our failure to fully trust God. As believers, we have this assurance from Psalm 9:10 which says, "And those who know Your name put their trust in You, for You, O LORD, have not forsaken those who seek You."

If we know God is with us, why do we still experience feelings of insecurity, doubts, and fears? Why does God seem so far away? In satan's arsenal, one of his biggest weapons is doubt. He loves for us to question who we are and how we measure up to others. He wants us to feel insecure over the meaning and purpose of our lives, where we're going, and how we'll get there.

True security comes when you recognize that God will supply everything that we need. When struggling with feelings of insecurity, never forget God's promises.

"Be careful for nothing; but in every thing by
prayer and supplication with thanksgiving let
your requests be made known unto God."
—PHILIPPIANS 4:6 KJV

"So we say with confidence, "The Lord is my helper; I will
not be afraid." What can mere mortals do to me?"
—HEBREWS 13:6 NIV

"He that dwelleth in the secret place of the most High
shall abide under the shadow of the Almighty."
—PSALM 91:1 KJV

"But he said to me, "My grace is sufficient for you, for
my power is made perfect in weakness." Therefore I
will boast all the more gladly about my weaknesses,
so that Christ's power may rest on me."
—2 CORINTHIANS 12:9 NIV

"But whoever listens to me (Wisdom) will live securely and in
confident trust. And will be at ease, without fear or dread of evil."
—PROVERBS 1:33 AMP

32

Facing a Crisis

G OD IS ABOVE OUR TROUBLE. He sees it in Divine per-
spective. God's help does not mean that his people are
kept from crisis, but that he keeps us through crisis.

David asked God for the eyes of faith to see with God's
clarity so he will not be overwhelmed with despair. At the
end of his prayer, David is reminded of the loving-kindness
of God.

Our God, as our refuge and strength, doesn't only get us
through crisis, but even gives us joy in crisis.

> *"These things I have spoken unto you, that in me ye
> might have peace. In the world ye shall have tribulation:
> but be of good cheer; I have overcome the world."*
> —JOHN 16:33 KJV

> *"Do not let your hearts be troubled. You believe in God; believe
> also in me. My Father's house has many rooms; if that were not
> so, would I have told you that I am going there to prepare a place*

*for you? And if I go and prepare a place for you, I will come back
and take you to be with me that you also may be where I am."*
—JOHN 14:1–10 NIV

*"Be always on the watch, and pray that you may be
able to escape all that is about to happen, and that
you may be able to stand before the Son of Man."*
—LUKE 21:36 NIV

33

Walking in Love

JUST AS CHILDREN like to imitate their parents, we are to mimic God in the same way Jesus copied His Father's behavior. We walk in love by imitating God just like Jesus did, offering our lives in sacrifice to God. We walk in love when we act like God.

When we behave like Jesus, we are walking in love. When we walk in love, we show the world that we are true followers of Jesus Christ. Our love for one another will prove to the world that we are His disciples.

"Follow God's example, therefore, as dearly loved children and walk in the way of love, just as Christ loved us and gave himself up for us as a fragrant offering and sacrifice to God."
—EPHESIANS 5:1–2 NIV

"For God so loved the world, that he gave his only begotten Son, that whosoever believeth in him should not perish, but have everlasting life."
—JOHN 3:16 KJV

*"But anyone who does not love does not know God,
for God is love. God showed how much he loved us
by sending his one and only Son into the world so
that we might have eternal life through him."*
—1 JOHN 4:8–9 NLT

*"If I give all I possess to the poor and give over my body to
hardship that I may boast, but do not have love, I gain nothing.
Love is patient, love is kind. It does not envy, it does not boast,
it is not proud. It does not dishonor others, it is not self-seeking,
it is not easily angered, it keeps no record of wrongs. Love does
not delight in evil but rejoices with the truth. It always protects,
always trusts, always hopes, always perseveres. Love never fails."*
—1 CORINTHIANS 13:3–8 NIV

*"A new commandment I give to you, that you love one another,
even as I have loved you, that you also love one another."*
—JOHN 13:34 NIV

34

Prayer

JUST LIKE YOUR PARENTS here on earth, your Heavenly Father wants to hear from you and talk to you. When you pray. For some people, prayer is simply a religious ritual. However, prayer can be much more than that—it is a way to get closer to God and improve our relationship with Him.

God always has a plan for us, but sometimes it can be challenging to understand. Praying helps us understand His will and accept it because His plans are always for our own good. Jeremiah 29:11 says, *"For I know the plans I have for you,' declares the Lord, 'plans to prosper you and not to harm you, plans to give you hope and a future."*

"Pray without ceasing. In every thing give thanks: for this is the will of God in Christ Jesus concerning you.
—I THESSALONIANS 5:17–18 KJV

"Therefore I tell you, whatever you ask for in prayer, believe that you have received it, and it will be yours."
—MARK 11:24 NIV

*"Therefore confess your sins to each other and pray
for each other so that you may be healed. The prayer
of a righteous person is powerful and effective."*
—JAMES 5:16 NIV

*"Watch and pray, that ye enter not into temptation:
the spirit indeed is willing, but the flesh is weak."*
—MATTHEW 26:41 KJV

"Continue in prayer and watch in the same with thanksgiving."
—COLOSSIANS 4:2 KJV

35

Victory Is Mine

JESUS WON an extraordinary triumph over sin, death, evil, poverty, illness, demonic powers, and so much else at the cross. He defeated those things and the enemy who is behind them. From what He did for us, we're meant to receive benefits. Our fate is not supposed to be living in a beaten down state constantly. Life has its troubles, but in Jesus Christ, we can meet them and defeat them.

Victory is the result of pushing through, by faith, all that would keep us from walking in the truth of God's word. As believers, we know that whatsoever is born of God overcomes the world. And the victory that has overcome the world is our faith.

> *"And this is the confidence that we have in him, that, if*
> *we ask any thing according to his will, he heareth us: And*
> *if we know that he hear us, whatsoever we ask, we know*
> *that we have the petitions that we desired of him."*
> —I JOHN 5:14-15 KJV

*"For the Lord your God is He who goes with you, to
fight for you against your enemies, to save you."*
—DEUTERONOMY 20:4 AMP

*"Wherefore take unto you the whole armour of God, that ye may
be able to withstand in the evil day, and having done all, to stand."*
—EPHESIANS 6:13 KJV

*"What then shall we say to all these things? If God is for us,
who can be [successful] against us? He who did not spare
[even] His own Son, but gave Him up for us all, how will He
not also, along with Him, graciously give us all things?"*
—ROMANS 8:31–32 AMP

*"O death, where is thy sting? O grave, where is thy
victory? The sting of death is sin; and the strength
of sin is the law. But thanks be to God, which giveth
us the victory through our Lord Jesus Christ."*
—I CORINTHIANS 15:55–57 KJV

P.O. Box 453
Powder Springs, Georgia 30127
www.entegritypublishing.com
info@entegritypublishing.com